she's strong, but she's tired

she's strong, but she's tired

r.h. Sin

Andrews McMeel
PUBLISHING®

your intro.

I don't want this for you, that pain you're feeling now. You're anxious to the point of opening this book, and here we are. We always meet this way, don't we? You, tired and weary from loving the wrong person, and me, the stranger who wants nothing but an opportunity to remind you that you matter. And you've given me that chance by deciding to pick up this book, by choosing to let me in. There have been moments when you feel like giving up on yourself, and so you elect to remain in a relationship that is no longer worthy of your energy and time—struggling to smile beneath the weight of your sadness. I may not know you, but I am familiar with the heartache that resides within your heart. I can recall being broken by someone who I thought could care for me. She up and decided to make a mockery of the energy and time I invested, just like he has done to you or maybe she has done to you. No matter the reason for your pain and who may have caused it, you are more than the fucked-up things that have happened to you, and you deserve more than what those fucked-up people gave to you.

It says a lot that you're here. Your eyes scanning this page with a heavy heart and mind that often feels confused and conflicted and tired, overthinking yourself into a corner that makes it difficult to walk away. You're here because you're ready to accept the fact that the person you love is incapable of reciprocating what you've given to them. You're here because the person you've fought for has done nothing but fight you instead of fighting for you. You picked up this book in search of a sign, not knowing that it would appear so early and even though it hurts like hell. The path to heaven on Earth usually begins with walking away from anyone who isn't supporting your idea of what love can be. And I admire you for that. Your ability to recognize your need and desire for more has inspired me to write down these very words. And though I am a bit unaware if these words will reach you in time, at least they're here, scattered upon this page for your eyes to see and for your heart to feel.

May your light shine brighter than it's ever been, despite the darkness that surrounds you, and may your heart pulsate a melody that feels like love, despite you feeling hated by the one you love. May your mind be at ease as you consume these words. I hope you find something here that encourages you to see more of yourself, and once you find more of who you are, I hope you understand more of what you deserve. I hope you never settle again. Because there is wild magic living within your heart, and most of the people you meet will indeed have no clue what to do with it, but I believe you will find the person who will know how to love you correctly. That journey can begin now if you allow it.

———————

be here now

be like the sun

you need no permission

to exist, to rise, to shine

be like the moon

make the choice

to light your path

in the depths of darkness

many forms of abuse.

he wants you to allow him back

into the heart he destroyed

he wants you to love him blindly

as if he didn't show you

time and time again

that he was unworthy of your love

he wants you to trust him

with your whole heart

despite knowing that he's betrayed you

breaking a woman down

only to return to her later

is a form of emotional abuse

———————

he is not sorry

forgive him

for the sake of yourself

and walk away

for the sake of your future

———————

women are poems

that write themselves

———————

it worked for a while

because you were empty

and he was full of beautiful lies

single mothers.

just because you share a child

doesn't give him domain over your life

just because he's the father of your child

doesn't mean you are obligated

to allow him the power to dictate your emotions

there is a way for him to father his child

without compromising your peace of mind

set boundaries, set rules

be the Queen that you are

and demand that he follow

those guidelines

just because you share a child

doesn't mean you have to share yourself

or share in part of his misery

———————

precious wild woman

chasing light, chasing love

———————

she stopped demanding him
to do all the things he wouldn't do
she stopped begging him to change
and just left him where he stood

———————————

Sadly, the world made her feel guilty for
wanting to leave a man who could never
appreciate her heart. She worried about quitting
on someone who gave up on her long ago.

It hurts because you genuinely give a fuck.
Sometimes the heart cares for the wrong person.

———

The right person will feel like home. So, keep moving until you find a safe place to rest.

―――――――――

You can't lose a man who never deserved to have you.

You can't find safety in the arms of a man who is the reason for your heartache.

the verge of.

How do you bear the heavy weight of sadness as
you struggle in silence. Telling others that you're
okay while the foundation beneath your house
of a heart begins to crumble and sink. You've
tried everything, it seems, and none of it works,
and so you travel down a road covered in shards
of broken hearts, the ones he broke before.you
even knew him. A history of disappointment, a
long list of events that would otherwise be red
flags if you had known who he truly was. But
he initially gave you the fraudulent version of
himself. He made promises to your heart that
he was never strong enough to keep, and in the
end, all of this made you feel weak. Too tired
to walk away but too tired to try again. You're
somewhere in the middle of loving him and on
the verge of loving yourself enough to leave him
behind.

———————

an abundance of self-respect

will cause you to detach

from friends who are secretly foes

and family members

who do nothing but harm your heart

the more self-respect you gain

the more willing you are to lose

people who don't deserve

to be kept

high frequency.

It was always his insecurities that made him unfaithful, that and his inability to stand firm in his commitment to the relationship. It takes a great deal of discipline and power to be able to devote oneself fully, and he found difficulty with the idea of remaining true to you. I know it hurts, knowing that the person you love will never be able to reciprocate the energy and care that you've given to them, but it's not a loss for you. Maybe one day he'll look back and wish he had done things differently, or perhaps he'll always be a fool, continually losing the things that should matter most to him. Regardless of what happens, you will go on to love yourself, and someone who matches your frequency will eventually love you.

in the end, you realize

you never needed him

he never deserved you

and so his absence

is not a loss

you gain so much more

when you remove people

who don't belong in your life

a concern of mine.

Sometimes I worry about you, the stranger
reading these words in this book. The stranger,
fighting a war by yourself. It's not easy being
you, but you do it to the best of your abilities.
It's not easy being you, and yet you survive on
nights like this. You inspire me so much, despite
being a stranger. You inspire these words as
you continue to fight for the love you deserve.
I know it feels like moving on is impossible,
and sometimes you don't even know where to
start, but I hope you know that there is a power
that lives within you. A power that no one can
destroy. A power that can be used to set yourself
free. Sometimes I worry about you, but then I
remember how strong you are. I believe in you,
and please believe in yourself.

single mothers II.

And to those of you coparenting a child with
a man who has been less than kind, create
boundaries, rules, guidelines. You deserve to be
respected, and he must know that, and he must
follow your rule as the Queen you are. You don't
have to walk away entirely from him, but you
mustn't allow him the power to dictate your life.
You are in control. Having a child in common
doesn't mean you're obligated to put up with
someone's b.s.

—————————

Stop giving second chances to fools. Stop providing new opportunities to those who never deserved a chance in the first place.

always this powerful.

Look how far you've come, despite the pain, the heartache. You continue, toward the love you deserve. You've always had this power, but there are nights when you're just tired. Weary from fighting, exhausted from being weighed down by toxic relationships. We may not know each other, but if you're here, you're important, and you matter, and I care, and I will always be here to remind you, to push you, to encourage you. Please, never give in or give up on yourself.

I think you're more than capable of doing what is necessary. No matter how difficult, you hold the required power to set yourself free. I don't want you to hurt anymore, and I hope these words help.

he needs to know.

If you're incapable of being faithful, don't waste
her time. If you're too weak to choose her and
only her, don't waste her time. If you're not
brave enough to love her for all that she is, don't
waste her time. She's evolving, and if you can't
support and encourage that, don't distract her.
Stay out of her way.

———————————

it is not up to you to keep an unkept man

it is not your job to fight for a man

who is too weak to respect and love you

———————

eyes filled with a wild flame

heart ruled by an appetite to love

you went searching for a soul mate

and found more of yourself

——————

you who made my soul ache

under the weight of disappointment

and betrayal

you who made me wait for a love

that you were never willing to give

he made you cold

then complained

about the weather

———————————

your ideas of love

molded by people

who pretended to care

molded by individuals

who were only out to use you

your ideas of love

tainted by fools

too weak to appreciate

your presence

dying to live.

and all this time
she was dying to live
and hating herself
for loving the wrong person
who pretended to be right

those days, those nights
fighting an unwinnable war
with an unbeatable foe

telling herself
that if she tried harder
things would change

———————

lying to herself

when he refused to be better

blaming herself

claiming that her standards

were too high

lowballing herself

just to keep him in her life

i don't think the pain

ever leaves

it lives and lives until you find

the courage to recycle it into strength

_____

they're too focused

on your flower

to ever truly appreciate

the strength of your roots

————————————

where does love really go

when given to the wrong person

coldest summer.

The air is cold in her heart, and ice is being made where she kept her love for you. I think you believed that she would give you another chance, not realizing that she had reached a point of no return. She is changing the locks, boarding up the windows to her soul. No longer willing to play your silly games, no longer willing to pretend to be okay with you crossing lines and tearing into her heart with no regard for what she's feeling. She brought about winter in the middle of summer. She found the courage to freeze you out.

———————

you don't win by playing the game

you conquer the players

by ignoring their existence

refusing to give them energy

———————

he says nothing when he speaks

there is no meaning behind his words

all those empty promises

and failure to follow through

you've lost so much time

believing in his lies

many years spent on a fool

who had only proven

to be good at being the worst

———————

his absence

no longer

made her ache

ready to be alone

willing to be without him

———————

You thought heartache would win, but you survived it.

———————

everything about him was fictional

a made-up character, a genuine fake

————————

she misses him

but she wants to forget

You're so distracted by how it ended that you don't even realize how wonderful it is to begin again on your own.

What you tolerate is what they'll continue to give.

The tiredness in her eyes, in her soul, and in her bones. Loving the wrong person is emotional exhaustion.

_____

I hope you find someone strong enough to be
soft with you and your heart.

---

it rains, and this is when you know

the sky is as sad as you are

_____

And you're just trying to be the only one they'll
ever love.

Removing people from your life is a symbol of self-respect.

The lowest version of a man is the one who texts
"I miss you" while lying in bed with the woman
he left you for.

———————

one day

her thoughts

will be beautiful

without sadness

and pain

some joy, some peace

and love

———————

but you're trying to give your heart
to someone who is only interested in your body

don't

———————

it's been years

and time has been unkind to you

your mind has been your biggest enemy

as you are forced to play back

things you wish to forget

i hope you find the peace you deserve

_____

replace him with yourself

you are greater than he is

sometimes the hurt is good

some damage becomes wisdom

some pain becomes strength

and you feel broken

but you are stronger than before

——————————

you need yourself more than you think

you deserve the love you've wasted on others

_____

and to think

you sink

because of him

and while drowning

you reach for his hand

you live in denial

you want to be saved

by someone who makes love

an unsafe place

she wore every face but her own

---

each scar is a confession of strength and survival

———————————

her heart is too pure

for the places it's been

———————

for once, she wanted

to be surprised

and not disappointed

but people are

who they've always been

pieces of shit

pretending to be gold

he left, and he should stay gone

he left

and so should you

———————

she's always thinking

about the feelings she hides

her pain hidden behind

a million "i'm okays"

still pretending to be fine

———————

this world

would feel incomplete

without you

keep fighting

keep surviving

keep living

please stay

"I miss you," she whispered while staring at her reflection. Looking for the woman she lost while loving someone incapable of caring for her heart.

you're extraordinary

stay away from mediocre men

who only wish to waste your time

_____

It's hard not to be loud about the things you genuinely love. Understand this when he decides to be silent about you.

Your life is a montage of survival and strength.
A story worth being celebrated.

It may not feel like it. But you are becoming a stronger version of who you've been. I know it gets difficult, believing in this idea that you are more than your brokenness.

———————————

your heart is broken

but true love will work

its way through the cracks

———————————

stop acting like you're weak

you are the definition of a powerful woman

on the verge of letting go and moving on

———————

be with someone who moves you

like the moon drifts through the night sky

you lose her trust

you lose your future

the sound of rolling thunder

rumbling its way through her heart

while a thousand fires burn

within her soul

wild, ember.

you are a wild ember glow

sparking the midnight sky

you roll like thunder

with flashes of lightning

inside your broken heart

you are a beautiful storm of fire

raging toward peace

running toward love

chasing what you deserve

July 22, 2019.

How could your birthday not matter to him?
Last year, he gave you nothing, and this year, he
forgot about you altogether. I guess I shouldn't
be surprised. Your life is filled with bumps and
bruises that he caused, due to not being there to
catch you whenever you'd fall. I watch our son
every day and wonder to myself, how could a
father and mother do so little for their kids? How
could a father leave his daughter vulnerable out
in the pasture with the wolves? And how could
your mother go absent, not there to teach you
how to have a presence? Luckily, you were able
to teach yourself how to cultivate and maintain
your magic. Luckily, you were strong when they
were weak, and I'm proud of you for being all
that you could be, even when they set you up to
fail.

beyond the fourth wall.

You're stuck between wanting to feel everything
and the desire to be numb. You want to be alone,
but you're afraid of the loneliness that might
arrive while you're on your own. You say you
want something real, but time and time again,
you've chosen to stay with someone who has
proven to be fraudulent in more ways than one.
It hurts, but you survive. You're in pain, and yet
you smile. You realize that moving on is your
best bet, but you've yet to access the courage
to leave. For some odd reason, you feel guilty
for wanting to let go. All in a while, the person
you're with doesn't feel guilty whenever they
hurt you. For so long, you've put others first
while allowing yourself to be secondary or never
chosen at all, and I think that it's past due that
you decide to choose yourself. I know you love
this person, but what's love in a relationship
with someone who treats you like they hate you,
and what's effort in a relationship with someone
who is never truly willing to try for you? There
shouldn't be an obligation to stay, but you feel
it. You feel it every time you're ready to walk
out of that door. It's torture. Waiting around for
something that may not happen, thinking they'll
change when they never will—dreaming of a
future with someone who feels more like a dead
end. Someone who will never be the person they
promised to be.

Who would you become if you left them right now? What would you do with the opportunity to pour more of your love into yourself? How would it feel to finally be in a position to receive real love from someone capable of appreciating all that you give? I need you to start asking yourself real questions like this. I need you to want more for yourself, because this relationship you've settled for is stale, confusing, and lacking whatever substance you'd need to feel loved. I'm not judging you. I completely understand why you've stayed for so long. You're strong enough to love unconditionally, you're devoted, and you're not one to quit, but isn't it hell, staying with the one who has abandoned you several times? Aren't you tired of being hurt when you should be loved for who you are and everything you have in your heart to share? You don't have to answer this right now, but all I ask is that when you put down this book that you begin to think about everything that occupies your time and begin to cut away the things that no longer fit into your present. You can't find love until you love yourself, and most times, the love of self will keep you on the path to a healthy relationship.

Fri 8:09pm.

I don't know when you'll read this or where you'll be when you find these words. Hopefully somewhere safe with someone who makes you happy, doing something that brings you peace. But if none of this is true for you, and you are to find these words amid heartbreak, I hope you know that you are fully deserving of a love that helps you grow. I hope you find a love that makes you forget about how painful it felt to love the wrong person.

———————

gracefully

she walked through

the storm

she never bowed

to the rain

―――――――――

it will be hard to leave

until it gets harder to stay

Because women don't always know that men often send those same texts to several women at a time, it's almost as if they go fishing with lies as their bait, hoping to get a bite. He wants you to feel special, and maybe you do. Maybe that text expressed everything you've been wanting to hear. Maybe that message arrived at the right moment, but it's designed to be and feel that way. How many times have you received an "I miss you" text from someone who ended up hurting you once more?

I think it's interesting that after you get your heart broken, your friends suggest that you go out and surround yourself with the same type of people who will hurt your heart. You go out to a club that is filled with individuals who mirror the same characteristics as your ex, while attempting to have fun in a room that is occupied by people who may be harmful for your soul. You want to feel better, and despite that temporary high you get while pretending that everything is okay, you've put yourself in an environment that will almost certainly cause you to repeat the same mistakes and possibly force you into another situation that resembles the relationship you were trying to move on from. Just a thought, something to think about.

———————

You can't keep giving your attention, time, energy, and love to a person who isn't willing to work for those things. Trying harder for someone who isn't willing to give you the least bit of their energy will just make you feel stuck.

—————————

Truth is . . . you're going to go through hardship before it gets any easier. You're going to go through pain before you can reach bliss. Don't give up on the peace and love you know you deserve. Please keep going.

in position.

Heavy manipulation, the way he makes you feel
bad for demanding what you deserve. You're
not clingy for wanting to be loved. You're not
nagging when trying to hold him accountable
for his actions. You're not asking for too much
when you insist that he makes the same amount
of effort as you've made. You don't have to feel
guilty for wanting to be chosen. You don't have
to feel bad for wanting to leave behind someone
who isn't willing to do much to make you stay.
Don't allow him the power to make you feel
like you're overreacting when all you're asking
for is respect and love. There's nothing wrong
with wanting to feel like you matter in your
relationship.

I hate that you've allowed them to silence you.
You walk on eggshells just to appease someone
who has never actually considered how you
may feel in this particular relationship. And you
continue to settle because you're afraid of losing
a person who doesn't even deserve to keep you.
And the longer you hold on to that person, the
more you lose yourself. I'm not judging you
for staying, I get it. You don't want to give
up on someone you love, but energy invested
into a toxic relationship is energy wasted. You
have two choices in the end: Hold on to the
one person who will destroy any hopes of you
knowing what true love feels like, or choose
yourself and pour all that you have into your
own peace of mind. Choose yourself because,
right now, you are deserving of the love you've
wasted on others. Choose yourself and you'll
be in position for something beautiful to finally
happen.

———————

stop providing your light

to people who push you toward darkness

But isn't that the problem? You put others first
and end up coming in last because you do more
for others than they'll ever do for you, and as
much as you think that this makes you a good
person, it doesn't. How can you be a good
person when you're so unkind to yourself?
How can you be so good to others and yet so
neglectful to yourself at the same time? The
only reward in helping those who will never
help you is a life that is filled with regret and
loneliness. One day you'll look back and wish
you lived instead of living a life of doing for
others.

———————

Your father half-asses everything, but you accept it. Maybe this is why you've settled for mediocre relationships with men who are only capable of giving a half-ass love, if any at all.

The same man who was supposed to protect you
left you with no shield, no sword, and so you
were tasked to fight off the wolves with your
bare hands. There's no shame in admitting that
you lost a few of those battles, but the irony of it
all is that your father left you vulnerable to men
who were just as weak as he is.

Life is beautiful when you begin to say no to all the people who were never worthy of a yes.

———————

Stop searching for closure from a man who wasn't even capable of comprehending your worth and love.

———————

Love me as if there is no one else you'll ever
need or want

Your relationship is shelter, your partner is a home. Some are beautiful cabins, homes that could house a family, lofts, skyrises, or mansions, while others are run-down places with faulty wiring and roofs that leak whenever it rains. What type of relationship are you in? What type of home is your partner?

———————

your soul is unsettled

your eyes wander recklessly

through the darkness

in search of light

your heart is aching

but no·one knows why

you are beautiful

an all-powerful being

with magic rushing

through your veins

in the silence.

i hear her

silently sitting there

wearing a smile

that dreadful mask

hiding her truth behind soft lips

and bright eyes

that appear to be sad

i hear her

saying nothing

silent screams

blister the air like winter

she sits still like cold air

frozen in sadness

pretending to be happy

i hear her

because i care

i hear her

i wish to listen

You

It's after 10 in the evening, and you've been glancing at your phone every three minutes, awaiting a notification or vibration as an indication that he has finally responded to that text message you sent hours ago. You've become so anxious waiting patiently for him to reach out to you. You're always texting first, you're always the one to reach out. You're always the one in waiting, as it would seem that he prefers to take his time and reply whenever it's convenient for him.

Eleven rolls around, and you're still sitting there. You begin to create a text, then after a brief moment of thought, you decide to delete the text. You don't want to seem clingy, needy, or overeager, but let's be honest: you wonder what the fuck he could be doing that is keeping him so busy that he's not able to respond. It's noon, and you receive a text from him. It's short, one-worded, non-enthusiastic, as always, and once your phone vibrates to show that you have one incoming text, you're excited a little, but you're also upset. Feelings of neglect have already taken their toll on you, and you're merely uncertain, angry, curious, but still a bit glad that he decided to reach out.

Him

He saw your text. He looked at your text earlier
that day and decided not to respond. His friends
are always bragging about the woman they
keep waiting. They live by this code of making
a woman wonder, forcing her to feel confused.
They never really want women to know how
much or how little they like them. It's part of a
game, a game they've learned to play well. Give
her enough to cause her to catch feelings, give
her just enough of your time, then pull away,
leaving her to pine and sit anxiously awaiting a
response. He looked at your text, then decided
at that moment how many hours he'd let pass
before responding.

He waited because he knows you'll wait around
for him, no matter what, or at least that's what
he thinks. See, you're just not that important,
you're not a priority in his life. And to top it all
off, he texted you at that hour, the exact hour
in which you'd given up hope that you'd get a
response, because his girlfriend is finally asleep.
Once she's asleep, he's free. He's free to waste
your time.

Morning arrives, and the cycle continues
because you don't know. But now you do,
and now it all makes sense. You are being
sent to voice mail when you call. He's always
unreachable, he's rarely consistent, and he never
seems to get "that text message" or somehow
doesn't have a chance to text you at a reasonable
hour. There's no time for you because his time is
invested elsewhere, but at least you know now.
At least you have the answer to your questions.
Stop entertaining those who refuse to make an
effort as far as you're concerned.

After you've been hurt, everything then becomes "too good to be true." You meet someone who makes you happy, and yet you act as if you're afraid of this newfound joy because of a situation within your past when that joy turned out to be nothing, but you can't allow your past to keep you from moving forward and into a better future with someone new.

The only way to discover if it's real is to let go of that nagging thought that "this is too good to be true." Stop cheating yourself because of your past and start treating yourself to a brighter future. Take chances, and love will find its way to you.

———————

you're beautiful

something you refuse to believe

you're good enough

something they fail to tell you

you deserve better

sounds cliché, but it's true

i've observed so many strong, real, intelligent,
and loyal women

put up with behaviors that are beneath them

your smile becomes a mask, your laughter
neglected . . .

your happiness on life support, nearly dying
because you've settled

for less than you deserve

Please don't let him make you feel guilty for wanting to be cherished and loved.

————————

i know you wish to hold on

you're afraid of letting go

you're hoping for change

but change will not arrive

do not water dead flowers

do not stay where you aren't loved

———————————

too often you distract yourself

with a new relationship

you smile to keep from crying

you do so much pretending

but you are not healed

———————

honest enough to say i miss you

strong enough not to take you back

———————————

of course, he'll live without you

but he'll eventually die one day

without knowing the magnitude

of the love you were trying to give him

before he betrayed your trust

he broke her heart

then complained

that she was heartless

———————

i don't think she's cold

i just think she's smart enough

not to waste her warmth on you

————————

give me a love

that never grows tired

give me a love

that isn't compromised by time

she built her own wings

she mastered the art of flight

and she flew above and over

anyone who wished to keep her grounded

———————

she wasn't sad anymore

yes, it was dark, but she made her own light

and found her way back to herself again

that was her magic

the way she loved

like she'd never been hurt

and sometimes she hides

because she knows that the one

who truly loves her

will see everything she's locked away

———————

it's hard, you know

training your lips to smile

while your heart is falling apart

they chase stars

but you are the moon

bigger, brighter

and nothing in the night sky

compares to you

you are worth

the attention

and devotion

they're not giving you

saying no to him

meant saying yes

to yourself

something about her

feels like a prayer

she embodies all the things

that i would hope for

she felt like breaking

but fought instead

you are a universe

of possibilities,

and it's a shame

he couldn't see it

———————

your pain is your candle

you learn your strength

by getting hurt

Don't get me wrong, the stars are beautiful;
but you, my dear, are more than that. You have
always been the moon in a pale-gray sky. Even
in darkness, you had more to love, more to see.
So much more to appreciate.

———————

no one is you

nothing and no one

can compete

burn some bridges

for light in the darkness

and for warmth in the winter

––––––––––

It's about time you started getting the type of
love and dedication you've wasted on others.

happy to be alone

is the woman

who has loved and been hurt

happy to be alone

is the woman

who would rather wait

for something real

than settle for something

that feels like nothing

———————

wanting him to be the one

is not enough to make him

worthy of you

———————

don't you need rest

after piecing every bit

of your heart back together

it's okay to take a permanent break

from choosing those

who won't choose you

———————

there were times

in which she felt alone

there were times

when all she wanted

was to fill that void

within her heart

there were times

when she just wanted

to share the things kept

sacred within her soul

there was a time

when she realized

that being alone

meant being available

to the one deserving

of her company

and this time

she's choosing herself

this time she's decided

that the path to true love

exists within

the night sky was her canvas

and she was the moon

supplying her own light

as she sat there alone

she was a Queen

without a King

she was royal

but by herself

still deserving

of the throne

and she refused

to settle for less

We judge women based on the ratio of ass, hips, and waist. We've literally turned them into numbers that are far less than their value. We objectify them so much that we're incapable of realizing what we have when in the presence of a good woman. Too lazy to dig deeper to find something within them that is truly rare and significant, we hop from woman to woman, searching, receiving what we think we want yet never truly satisfied.

And that's why we stay longer than we should, because it hurts to watch something you love transform into something you should hate, something that hurts your heart and soul. We sit and wait for it to return to its original state. We go through the pain of investing our hope into a hopeless situation, in denial as we ignore the fact that what we see was always there and what is now will always be. And so the heart begins to break. It shatters because you're not ready to move on, but you know you must move forward without the person you thought you needed.

Love is having someone beside you to confront your demons. Someone willing and ready to stand beneath stormy clouds with you and not be moved. Someone patient with your sadness while assuring you that things will get better. Love is out there, love lives within, and the romantic love you wish for will arrive. Never give up on your idea of what being in love means.

I'm just not who I was before you. I allowed you into a place untouched by the hands of anyone. I held the door open just so that you could walk in and make a home out of me. You took my willingness, my acceptance and destroyed the insides of my heart. You took the trust that I gave unto you and threw it away as if to say, "This is garbage." Before you, I was different. After you, I'll never be the same.

I'd rather you fall in love with the parts of me that no one cares to know. Only then would you truly understand what it means to love me.

———————

and that's your problem

you're too good at holding on

too strong to let go

too loyal to walk away

too kind to leave

even after he's abandoned you

you're too good at giving yourself

to someone too stupid

to see the true worth

in all that you do

and i hope you find the strength

to eventually choose yourself

it's time to be kinder

to your own heart

———————

I think she knew she'd have to let go, yet she
held on to parts of him that no longer existed.
There were times when she'd look into his eyes
and see nothing, times when he'd say, "I'm
sorry," and she'd force herself to believe it.
The arguing disguised as passion. The fighting
disguised as love. How is it that the man who
once pledged his allegiance to your heart is now
the one forcing you to pick up the pieces by
yourself after he broke it? And why are you so
willing to take him back even after he's proven
time and time again that he's not worth the love
you've given him?

we could have been great

but you insisted on being mediocre

you placed limits on us

and what we could be

so i chose myself

i deserved more

i chose me

instead of us

and that's when

the healing began

anger based.

What upsets me is that you smile in their faces while they laugh and joke about you behind your back. You make every effort to make them feel special, all while they overlook you as often as they can. They're supposed to be the ones to protect you from the coldness of this world, and yet they bring about winter in your heart. And even though you feel broken, you still love them with whatever you have left. That's what bothers me the most. Witnessing you give everything to a group of people who do nothing but disappoint you. And your only reason for allowing them to hurt you is because they're family.

self, safe.

Aren't you tired of feeling confused, abused
verbally by the same mouth that claimed to
love you? Only to leave your heart aching after
every argument you enter? You left the last
time feeling like less than you were before—
your self-esteem buried beneath a rubble of
uncertainty. You want things to get better, you
hope for change. You rearrange everything
about yourself to appease a person who isn't
concerned about your peace of mind. You find
time to give while they refuse to make time
for you. You are always fighting, not realizing
that using that energy on someone like this will
still amount to a losing battle. You ignore your
scars because they remind you that you should
move on. You see the stains on the wall, and you
decide to paint over them. You know the truth
and what you must do, but you move blindly into
love with no regard for your own heart. I wish
you knew of your own strength. I wish you'd
realize that it's time to keep yourself safe.

_____

she's committed to herself

she's devoted to finding the love

that lives within

————————

i wish your father tried harder

i wish more effort was placed into you

i wish he was more present

more loving, more protective

of your heart

i wish your mother tried harder

i wish more effort was invested into you

i wish she was more present

more loving, more protective

of your heart

the war and your survival.

How do you do it? How do you make it through
the type of nights that would drown others?
How do you survive the waves of unhappiness?
Sadness comes knocking at your door, and the
more you ignore it, the louder it gets as midnight
creeps toward your window, pushing the moon
higher than before. You're unreal, but you're
here, fighting amid the night sky and dreaming
beneath the light of the moon. You're unreal,
but you're here, a traveler in search of love and
understanding. You didn't set out to get hurt, but
it happened. But you continue to move forward,
and you refuse to give up. There are nights when
the darkness becomes overwhelming; the later
it gets, the more your heart seems to sink into
itself—such a terrible feeling, one that is hard to
explain. You scream into your pillow, your eyes
tightly shut. You are hoping that when you open
them and reemerge from the rivers of pain that
everything will be made different and you'll be
able to breathe freely again, even if it isn't. If all
remains the same and the heartache arrives at
the same time every night, you'll still do it, and
you'll still be here surviving. You'll still be here,
fighting yet another war. And I'll again wonder
how you do what you've always done.

hourglass.

When you think about it, there's so little time
to retrieve the love you say you want. So little
time that there's not much room for error, and
yet here you are. Feeling around in the dark for
a love that isn't even there. We always meet this
way, don't we? Your heart is broken, and so you
stumble upon my words intentionally. Looking
for yet another reminder as to why you should
leave the person you're with. It's been years now,
and your heart has felt this uneasiness for far too
long—longer than you deserve. I'll tell you to
move on, and you'll respond and say it's easier
said than done, and that saying will force you
into a cycle in which you decide to hold on to
one person who is no longer deserving of your
love. Moving on is easier said than done, but it
has never been impossible. This world is made
up of people who have decided that they deserve
more, and the only way to bring them closer to
a love that matters is to leave behind the person
who has made them feel like they don't matter.

Maybe these words will reach the person who is tired of fighting for someone who does nothing but destroy their happiness. Perhaps these words will reach the individual who has reached their breaking point and is ready to break free. Maybe these words will reach someone like you, a person who knows that they deserve so much more but has felt stuck in their relationship because of time invested and love given. You're reading this now for a reason, you picked up this book for a reason, and I know that you won't be able to leave overnight. I'm aware that it takes time, but don't waste the time you have left searching for real love in a fraudulent person. Don't waste whatever time you have left trying to love someone who has proven to be incapable of being strong enough to care for you in the way you need.

———————

move on

fuck him

be brave

Correct me if I'm wrong, but I think it hurts because you genuinely give a fuck. It hurts because even though you want to hold on, you know that letting go is the best thing you could do for your future, and that doesn't make it any easier.

when you begin

to search for real love

seek yourself

———————

she grew silent

like a flower in winter

he was no longer

worthy of her words

and so she said nothing

on her way out

the saddest eyes i've ever seen

belonged to a woman

surrounded by friends

in a nightclub

———————

be empty

then fill your heart

with more of yourself

———————

ignore what he said

observe what he does

remarkable

the way she collapses

yet catches herself

---

forever is fractured by lies and betrayal

———————

he's been your nightmare

wake up

———————

someone you need

is searching for you

———————

she understands the rain

because she too is used to falling

---

i am a victim of hoping

for something that can't happen

———————

you are worthy of your love

you are worthy of your forgiveness

you are worthy of your kindness

start choosing yourself

———————

her soul

a rainbow

of infinite vibrance

———————

she made herself at home

within her own arms

———————

you are allowed

to burn bridges

that no longer

deserve to reach you

———————

feel what you need to feel

say what lives within your heart

and never hold on to things

that don't belong in your life

he can't love you

like you love you

move closer to yourself

———————

she dreams of being loved

the way she loves

I'll say this. Never listen to anyone who tells you that real love doesn't exist. There are two versions of a broken heart. One where a person stops believing in love and one where a person continues forward in search of something real, no matter how hurt they may feel. I'm glad that my wife continued after heartbreak. I'm glad my wife never gave up on the idea of finding real love. If my wife believed that real love didn't exist, then we wouldn't have found each other. I'm looking at my son right now, and he's a representation of what happens when real love wins. It's so easy to give up on love after you've been betrayed many times, but for the ones who haven't lost hope . . . I can assure you that no matter how broken you may feel, there is someone in the world searching for someone like you. I had always been searching for my wife, and this is why I know love is real, and I don't believe that I'm the only man on this earth who is capable of loving one woman and reciprocating the love she gives me. Don't give up. Don't let heartbreak dictate your future and your beliefs. Don't give your ex that power.

8/22/19.

You're reaching for someone who is the cause
of your pain—reaching for someone who is the
reason that you're sinking, nearly drowning. You
put so much hope into a person who has often
left you hopeless. Do you not remember why
your heart is breaking? Do you not remember
why your soul is weary? Aren't you tired
of pretending to be happy when you're not,
pretending that this is love when it feels like
hate?

I'm tired of always being present in your absence. I'm tired of trying harder when you make no effort. I'm tired of giving a love that is never reciprocated—tired of forgiving you when you're not genuinely sorry. I'm tired of giving second chances when you never deserved the first. I'm tired of pretending that everything is fine while I continue to fall apart inside. I'm tired of being in love alone. I'm just tired.

I thank you when you've done nothing to help.
I praise you for all the things I wish you'd
do. I celebrate you even as you ignore my
accomplishments. I paint you with vibrance,
but you've always been a dull color, gray. I say
to myself, "Maybe it'll get better, I have to stay
longer to see it through," when honestly I should
look into your eyes and whisper, "Fuck you."

There are moments when I wish I had a time machine. I'd use it to go back to the moment we met and avoid you at all costs. Because being here with you has been a waste of my future.

———————

The only future you have by holding on to the
wrong person is a life that will never know what
it means to be loved truly.

———————

you are a needed phenomenon

like rain falling in the middle of the desert

and if he can't realize that your existence

can be summed up as a rare occurrence

then he doesn't deserve you

Tell me why you're crying, tell me why you decide to stay where you're not appreciated. Don't you remember what it felt like to be happy on your own, free from heartache? Free from him and his bullshit? Tell me why you've decided to settle, struggling to survive the impact of his disrespect and disregard for your emotional well-being. Are you crying because you wish to hold on longer, or is it that you're ready to let go but you're afraid?

———————

You will find everything you've ever needed in the absence of everyone who couldn't appreciate you.

Sometimes people can't comprehend the power of your love until it's taken away from them without an explanation.

I think you ought to be in love with yourself a little deeper.

———————

sadness leaves

but it never dies

―――――――――

it's been a long time

since you've chosen yourself

———————

the moon

is most visible

during darkness

and so is your strength

———————

whatever causes the rain

in your soul and the pain

in your heart

leave it behind

———————

sometimes you get better

sometimes you're just different

———————

when you dream of true love

i hope you dream of yourself

———————————

you want so many things

and you want it from

the wrong person

———————

her tears are full of ghosts

remnants of heartbreak

she's been through hell

but there's still heaven

in her bones

———————

midnight was nothing more than

a cemetery for dead stars

―――――――――――

if he loved you

he'd choose the peace

in your heart

instead of chaos and confusion

———————

you love him

you're just not willing

to allow yourself to stay any longer

because you refuse to let him hurt you

He knew he wasn't shit when he approached you. He knowingly wasted your time. He knew damn well that he was incapable of fully comprehending your worth, and even though that shit hurt you, even though your heart has been aching, soul weary, restless, unable to sleep, I hope you still remember what you're worth, and I hope you take all the energy and love and time that you've invested in him and give it entirely to yourself. I hope this reaches you, the one who needs this the most.

————————————

it almost feels as if

your puzzle piece isn't meant

to fit anyone

but you keep going

you keep loving

and that's brave

———————

Go someplace where you feel free. Far away from him and his bullshit. Someplace where your soul can finally be at ease.

Love isn't supposed to feel terrible. Love is
supposed to destroy the most terrible things.

You're almost there, just a little bit longer now.
Keep your head up, guard your heart, and love
yourself through this storm.

Sometimes I don't want to be human. Aching
for something that I can never find, empty
from giving my all without any of it being
reciprocated. Falling in love alone then forced to
pick up the pieces of my own heart. Who wants
to be human when it hurts this much?

———————

Something good happening with someone good
enough to love me in the way I need.

———————————

never mind the summer

if you wish to find winter

look into my soul

and i once thought

feeling nothing was safer

until being numb

kept me from finding you

scene fifty-two.

This life, your life. You've done so much of it alone. You've carried yourself through flames, you've reached for your own hand successfully while drowning. You're remarkable even when you won't believe it. No cape, just strength. The power to hold yourself up whenever you fear falling. Instead of looking to others, you save yourself. You are the hero you've always needed. You are the hero you deserve.

your reality.

I was watching this reality show with my wife
the other night. It's a show that profiles the lives
of strangers getting married, and the viewer gets
the opportunity to witness two people attempt to
cultivate and maintain a marriage. There was an
episode in which the guy, newly married to his
wife, began to stay out at all hours of the night,
sometimes returning days later. We watched the
wife nearly torment herself while pacing back
and forth in their apartment and sending texts
that were ignored. Phone calls sent to voice
mail, a heart aching because it felt neglected. All
of this happened, and when he finally returned
home, though she was upset, she found a way to
excuse his behavior just enough to feel the need
to reward him.

This got me to thinking about you, the person
reading this now. How many times have you
made excuses for someone who hurt you? How
many times have you ignored the screaming
truth, just so that you could feel justified
in giving that person another opportunity
to disappoint you? I think the world and its
teachings have been so unkind to the mind of
women, instructing them to do more when the
people in their lives do nothing—teaching them
to feel bad about demanding what they deserve,
being made to feel like you're asking for too
much when it comes to being loved and feeling
loved. It hurts me to think that someone can
mistreat you, break your heart, and you could
still love them with every piece of you scattered
across the floor.

I'm not judging you. I want the best for you. I want you to know what it means to be fully appreciated. Life is too short to be in a relationship that feels like hell. A relationship that drains and destroys you. Why are you so hard on yourself and so easy on someone who never makes it easy for you?

definitively you.

Define your value, take power away from others
who wish to treat you as if you're not good
enough. Understand your worth and demand
that you be treated with respect and love. Be
ready to walk away from the people who prove
to be unworthy of standing beside you. Stop
giving second chances to individuals who did
nothing but disappoint you from the first, and
start choosing yourself. Especially while feeling
overlooked by those you care about the most.
Understand that you are not obligated to stay
in any relationship that isn't encouraging you
to grow. Understand that you do not have to
feel bad about wanting what you give; there's
nothing wrong with demanding what you
believe you deserve. It's time to take control of
your future by placing certain people in your
past.

———————————

I wonder if your shadow grows weary of you
dragging it into relationships that were never
worthy of your presence.

———————

It's like the longer you hold on to the wrong person, the further you are from the type of relationship you feel you deserve.

Heartbreak will alter the way you feel about relationships, but don't let the pain keep you from discovering the right person to love.

You fear being alone, and so you've chosen to
be with the one who makes you feel the most
lonely. You want to be loved, but you've decided
to hold on to one who seems to hate the idea of
you being happy.

Choosing yourself means deciding to be happy, despite your feelings for the wrong person.

Choosing yourself means giving yourself a second chance at peace.

some will fall

you will stand

————————

the pain you feel now

is not your forever

———————

You've had this terrible feeling living inside your bones, and it's time to listen to what the aches are trying to tell you.

For you, beauty is much more than the surface. Beautiful is the way you fight for what you deserve. Beautiful is how you survive feeling broken.

She was tired emotionally, but she had just enough left to move on with her life.

she sounds like music

the sound of a song

that symbolizes a devotion to herself

———————————

one day you'll make sense

to the only one strong enough

to hear the pain behind your silence

―――――――――

Give up the person who forced you to give up
your smile.

Maybe the one you're supposed to be with is
distracted by the wrong person also.

Be kinder to the woman crying back at you in the mirror.

scene fifty-three.

I honestly wish I could do more for you, and I
wish there were magic words that I could spell
out that would assist you in breaking free from
the bondage of being with someone whose only
intention is to use and abuse you. I've read back
over so much of the content in this book, and I
genuinely hope that my intentions were not lost
and that maybe you found something that could
motivate you to move forward with your life.
But still, I wish there were more that I could do
for you. To the heart that is breaking, the soul
that is weary, and the mind that is currently
struggling with the idea of detaching from the
person you believed would reciprocate the love
you've given to them: maybe you're reading
this in search of an answer. An answer that I'm
not sure that I have. But whoever you are and
whenever you get the chance to read this, I hope
you find the magic in letting go. I hope you
discover the reward for moving on.

I want you to know that, despite the heartache
that has always filled your heart, and even
though you're used to being hurt, you still
deserve a love that doesn't cause you anguish.
You still deserve a love that is everlasting and
true. I get it, you've been with the wrong person
for so long that you've nearly given up on this
idea of true love. You've decided to stay because
of the time and energy you've invested, but
imagine if you gave that same time and energy
to someone capable of reciprocating the things
you throw their way. Imagine how peaceful it
would be to find someone who considers you
always.

It just happens. You don't plan for it, but when it happens, you embrace the idea with an open mind. It's so good in the beginning, that feeling of perfection. Ignorance is bliss, and that feeling of bliss can cause you to be blind to the reality of what may be happening. Time becomes your energy because the more you invest, the closer you are to figuring out that the love you believed to be real may have just been a manipulative lie. Empty promises made in an effort to make you vulnerable enough to share the energy they never deserved. It just happens that way, and it happens to the best of you—the best of us.

You've been running from yourself lately, afraid
of what will happen when you finally catch
up. Change can be a scary thing, but you must
never pass up the opportunity to grow. You're
evolving into everything they said you'd never
be, and that's beautiful. That is a change worth
embracing.

Despite the change in the weather, despite the storm, she went on growing, blooming, and becoming more of everything she was meant to be.

I can't fault you for wanting to walk away from people who fail to respect you, and no, I don't think you should feel bad for distancing yourself from them.

broken girls

keep poems

inside their hearts

that should be celebrated

and revered

you can reach for others

you can hope that they save you

or you can reach for yourself

because in the midst

of needing to be saved

the only arms long enough to reach you

the only hands strong enough

to protect you are yours

———————

be your own companion

while you wait to be loved

by someone other than yourself

Stop holding on to what you should have left behind.

You never belonged to him. Don't let him own
your emotions.

———————————

pain seals itself in our tears

cry because that's the way

toward the freedom to feel joy

—————

You're trying to fit real feelings into a fraudulent relationship. Stop.

the moon knows her name

midnight keeps calling

answer below.

How much of night do you waste on thinking about what you could have done better in a relationship with someone who refuses to even try? How much of midnight have you used to hide your tears behind a shade of black? How much are you willing to lose in a relationship that drains you so much that you don't even have the energy to sleep? How long will you stay with someone who will never grow?

———————————

Remind yourself that you deserve better by letting go of the person who doesn't deserve you.

You're built for this. The part where fear creeps up into your mind whenever you think about leaving or the pain that arrives when trying to survive the breakup. You're built for the heartache, and you have the strength to get through it. The courage to move on lives within you, use it.

How is it that you feel bad about leaving him,
but he never gives a fuck about hurting you?

Purge the idea of him from your heart by accepting the fact that he's always been too weak to appreciate your presence.

You had greatness in you all along. You just had to find your fire.

_____

Find your fire and burn through everything that
no longer fits into your life.

You will wake up from this nightmare. You will dream-dreams worth dreaming when you detach from the things and the people who hurt you.

———————

Don't let a day go by without reminding yourself that you are worthy of a love that makes you feel safe.

What happens to your dreams when you can't
sleep.

Dear woman,

You're holding this book, reading these words.
I'm not sure where you are or what time it will
be at the moment you read this, but I know
your heart is heavy with pain and your mind
is filled with confusion. You've been holding
on to someone who was never worth it, loving
someone incapable of loving you back. You
stay because you've invested too much into this
relationship to leave, but as you read this, you
realize that, more than ever, it's time to let go.
I admire your patience, but life is too short to
wait around for someone to be something they
can't. I admire your strength, but instead of
using all you have to hold on, you have to use
that same strength to move on with your life.
We're strangers at this moment, and though we
may not know one another, I happen to know
what currently lives within your heart. I wish
you knew that there was magic living beneath
your bones. I wish you knew that you have
always been more than enough. I wish you knew
that you are strong enough to set yourself free.
Maybe this isn't enough, and perhaps you'll
miss this message. No matter what happens, I
can't give up on you, and I hope you don't give
up on yourself. These words were written for
the woman who is strong but tired. The woman
who sometimes forgets to choose herself. These
words are for the woman who, despite feeling
broken, decides to survive. It's time to walk
away, be brave.

Sincerely, a stranger who cares,

r.h. Sin

———————

you wear sadness as a winter coat

draped over your body so perfectly

hanging on to your shoulders for dear life

as it blows in the wind

they were never lovers

they never loved me

i tried to use them for warmth

but in the end, i shivered alone

in the cold of the night

And you were broken just as much I was. Our
scars similar, our wounds the same. Those sad
eyes were looking back at me as if I had the
answers, and even though I wish I had, I was
struggling just as much as you were. I was bored
with the overdone physical show of tainted
affection and the emptiness that occurred after
the act was over. We were searching for more,
and more brought us to each other. I still think
about that, and I spend sleepless nights lying
next to you, dreaming while awake of the
moment our brokenness pushed us into each
other's arms, and that's why, deep down, I'm
grateful for the pain. It all began not because
I was looking for a good fuck. I just wanted
someone to live a good life with.

---

you're afraid

that you're going to be

the only one who remembers

everything you wish to forget

old friends

new strangers

that's what we've become

———————————

be careful who you build

your dreams on

I know it's hard because you've been hurt so many fucking times, but you are worth finding. You are worth loving.

_____

the way you survive is art

you're becoming a masterpiece

peace dwells within you

and despite the chaos in this world

there is a calm wherever you go

there is bliss in your presence

Perhaps he was never what you needed, and you only believed in him because he was capable of telling you everything you wanted to hear whenever you needed to hear it.

Self-love is the best practice of affection.

I wish you could remember how it felt before he entered your life. I know you like to think that he was someone worth letting in, you believe whatever it is you need to help you hold on. You obsess over the good times, blurring out the bad. Ignoring the warning signs and red flags, but deep down, you know what you must do. Deep down, you're unhappy, and behind that smile is everything you've kept to yourself. And I wish you'd remember how happier you were before he decided to destroy your peace. I wish you could remember how to find the courage that has already lived within your heart, and more than anything, and I wish you knew that you'd be fine without him in your life. I know you've invested so much of yourself into him and the relationship, but you must understand that nothing will make a difference in a relationship with someone who would rather hurt you than love you. None of that will ever make a difference to someone who has always been too weak to stand beside you. I know you've dedicated your life to him, and for that, I dedicate these words to you. There is a goddess-like power that resides deep within everything that you are, and it is waiting to be used on your path to emotional freedom. It's time to break away from the man who will never deserve you.

I think you need to know that it is entirely okay to detach from members of your family who cause nothing but pain and discomfort in your life. I think it's okay for you to break up with family members who are toxic and disappointing. "Family" is not a word that should cause you to compromise.

You've been dancing around the truth for so
long that you've learned to move willingly
with the lies he tells you. And I wish you'd stop
allowing him to return when he never meant to
stay in the first place.

_____

while other poets wish

to only show off their ability

to use words you'll never understand

or to reference ideas too complex

for even themselves

i choose to speak to you

and your heart

while the other writers

are prisoners of their vanity

and pursuit of fame

i'm running after you

trying to prevent you

from throwing your life away

for a lover who will never love you

Maybe you don't give a fuck about what I have to say. Perhaps I'm too much of a stranger to matter to you, but that won't make me give up on this idea of you finally being happy on your own and in your relationship. I know moving on is easier said than done, but you are capable of walking away from anyone who refuses to choose you. Your heart has seen a fair share of heartache, but you always find a way to survive, and every time your heart breaks, you rise stronger than before. You're worth everything you've been wanting. You deserve a love that will help and encourage you to grow. It's time to choose yourself. It's time to break free. You are more than enough, and you are fully capable of freeing yourself. I refuse to give up on you. Please, don't give up on yourself.

she is a museum of wild art

strokes of strength

and courage on a canvas

———————

Make a list of what you want, need, and deserve.
Then remove people from your life who are
keeping you from everything on that list.

Consider that this life we lead is entirely too short, made shorter by the time we spend on people who were never worth our energy. You've already lost so much of your time as is, what sense would it make to give him more of you when he's never willing to appreciate all that it is you have to offer?

Blood may be thicker than water, but it will never be more important than peace of mind and joy within the heart.

A family is just a group of titles until the individuals in your family give more meaning to their roles by showing up when the time comes.

strangely familiar.

Sometimes I think of you, but not in the way
that others do. See, we're strangers, and what
that means is that I don't actually know your
name and maybe I don't know what you look
like, but that doesn't mean I can't deem you
familiar. You seem like someone so sad that
you smile often. You're one of those women
who search for love in all the places it'll never
exist. And no matter how large a heart you have
and no matter how much you give, none of it
seems to work, and because of this, you feel like
a failure. You feel like giving up on this idea
of true love because every relationship you've
entered has turned your heart a bit colder. And
so, sometimes I think of you. The thought
of you and what you're going through runs
through my mind like a tornado. This storm,
though powerful, is not one I run from but one I
willingly chase until I feel as lost as you.

Don't you feel lost? Doesn't it feel like
everything you've wanted doesn't exist? Do you
feel like you're running toward a dead end, or
maybe you feel like there's no end in sight for
the heartache you feel? The nights drain you,
the nighttime sky a symbol for what you think—
struggling to find light beneath a half-moon.
You fight wars that no one will know about.
Your heart screams things no one will ever hear,
or at least you thought so. I want so badly for
you to read this. I need you to know that you are
not alone, and even in a crowded night, full of
hearts breaking just like yours, I feel you, and
sometimes I think of you.

All of everything you've ever given was always more than enough. You were giving it to someone incapable of comprehending all that you've ever been.

The heart is more honest at midnight when it is
too tired to lie to itself.

———————

Uncertainty has no place in a relationship. The confusion drains the heart of its energy to love.

He was never a loss. You learn this when you realize that his absence just gave you more time to love yourself.

The sad truth is that lonely people tend to choose others who will lead them to more loneliness.

———————

The love you imagined is real, just not with him.

you are rain

when the roots

need it most

you are light

in the silence

of midnight

———————

you feel sadness

but you are still worthy

you feel broken

but you are still powerful

———————

she still loves him

but she's no longer willing

to compromise her heart

―――――――――

if you wait for him,

you'll be furthest

from joy

if you hold on to him,

your heart will know nothing

but heartache and disappointment

his ghost lives in her tears

do not lose who you've been

to keep a man who will never

appreciate all that you are

the more you drown

the thought of him

the closer you drift

toward peace

in silence

we say a form of nothing

that means so much

———————

Right now, you wonder if you should stay, and
that alone is a sign.

———————————

some silence

is harsher

than screaming

———————

you are strange and wonderful

and i hope you find a love

that matches what you are

part one.

there are parts you'll never show

parts of you they'll never know

there's madness in your soul

but you smile through it

laughing at bad jokes

in an attempt to get through it

trying to find peace

but you often lose it

they claim to love you

but they'll never prove it

and moving on is difficult

easier said than done

until you do it

you're surprised

by how strong

you are

but I'm not, you're magic

and I always knew it

part two.

you danced in circles

you danced in the darkness

re-creating the midnight moon

and soon your shade

will become light

and at the same time

every morning you'll rise

like that tremendous big orb of light

you survive, and you shine

you fall, then get back up

you thrive

part three.

tell me the secrets

you've buried

show me the memories

you struggle to forget

tell me your regrets

show me what is hidden

no matter how difficult it gets

i want to see your misery

don't be ashamed

of what haunts you

the only way to defeat your devils

is to confront them

and you can do this on your own

or we can do this shit together

i'd gladly weather any storm

that comes for you

turn your loneliness into us

i'm not afraid of your demons

and i'll stay

because i love you that much

part four.

tainted love fades

just like shade

when the sun rises

a new day could be

your chance to find your strength

or it could be

another moment of misery

as you struggle to walk away

from all the things

that no longer bring you joy

what will the morning bring you

is it happiness, will it be painful

will you survive

or will it be too much

tainted love fades

but the love you give unto yourself

will always be more than enough

to get you through the heartache

part five.

i hope you're doing better

the letters stopped

you're not reaching out anymore

you've gone silent on me

and i can't help but worry about you

i hope these words find you

in your moment of need

and even though you may feel invisible

i hope this helps you feel seen

———————

I hope you see how beautiful it is to begin again
without the person you thought you needed.

You carry him and all of his bullshit, but tell me,
who carries you when you are too broken to go
on?

Not everyone leaves—just the ones who were never worthy of being by your side.

———————

Love yourself entirely, and stay away from anyone who loves you less than that.

———————

he offered her the stars

in exchange for her moon

and she said no

————————

I believe it hurts because you spent so much
time making plans. You invested so much time
while they were busy wasting it without you
knowing.

———————

a man in love

is motivated

to make sure

the one he loves

feels secure

in their relationship

plot twist, she was better without him

Sometimes your emotions are based on lies, and you fall for someone who only intended to break your heart. Don't trust everything you feel. Take your time and know the difference between someone making promises and someone carrying out all the things they've proclaimed.

———————

when you're truly in love

your soul will smile and not feel weary

I could already hear it in your voice, and you whispered, "I'm fine." All the while you were falling apart. They don't understand you, and you don't need them to in order to be happy. All that matters is that you are strong enough to feel whatever it is that lives within you, and that's how I know you'll be strong enough to survive. Keep going.

destroy some bridges.

I think it's okay to distance yourself from people
who keep you from feeling all the right things.
It's essential to make room for more moments
that grant the heart the opportunity to feel
loved and cherished. You cheapen your life by
allowing your heart to be invested in people
who break it. Sometimes it's not even a romantic
relationship. Sometimes the person you need
to break up with is a family member, maybe
a close friend. You are never obligated to stay
where your heart is unable to thrive. No matter
the title that person holds in your life, no one
should be allowed to break you down.

she cried

but this time

her tears

drowned away everything

that didn't belong

---

not all light is beautiful

you see, some light is blinding

in a way that keeps you

from seeing the entire truth

———————

you were never needy

you weren't asking

for too much

you demanded

what was necessary

for you to feel loved

and they were incapable

of meeting those demands

_____

ignore them

let them go

focus on your ph levels

drink more water

build your savings account

say no to everything

you don't want to do

do any and everything

that involves you

moving past their bullshit

because you are worth so much more

why stay in a relationship

in which you feel stuck

that's not how you grow

———————

so much of the pain

lives in the unspoken spaces

of the heart

moments wrapped in silence

out of fear of being judged

you've hidden so much

of yourself there

where no one sees

until now, until this very moment

don't be ashamed of what you feel

your pain is a part of your story

tell it without fear

There's always that one person who you feel like you can never give up on, and the fucked-up part about this feeling is that person has always given up on you so quickly.

———————

you need not unfold your heart

for anyone who isn't willing

to prove themselves worthy

of being loved by you

———————

Someone who takes risks to keep you, not.lose you.

———————————

the love you deserve

is far from ordinary

it doesn't hurt

it won't break you

don't settle

not weak.

First of all, you're not weak for staying. What you need to know is that it takes a great deal of strength to withstand the storm that is heartbreak. It takes a great deal of strength to hold on to a relationship that does nothing but destroy you, but that same power can be used to set you free.

I tell people to move on, and their response is often, "It's easier said than done," and though it's true, I also think it's just something people say to justify their choice to stay with someone who had already given up on them a long time ago. Sadly, you've gotten to a point where instead of fighting for your peace of mind, you'd rather stay with someone who treats you like a piece of shit, and I'm just one person who wants you to remember that you will survive without that person.

You think it's so hard to walk away, but imagine how hard it should be to give all of your love to someone who will never deserve you.

It's time to love yourself enough to walk away. It's time to love yourself so much that you no longer allow others the opportunity to hurt you. I need you to know that you are worth so much more than the relationship you've settled for. I need you to see who you've always been instead of the brokenness they've made you feel. You are more than the pain that resides in your heart.

I know I sound like a broken record, but I refuse
to give up on you. Sure, you can hate me, get
angry with me, or ignore these messages, but I'll
always be here for whenever you wish to listen,
to read, to consume these words. I want you to
be happy, because you deserve to have peace.

honor and devotion.

Before you could ever be faithful to someone, you must practice loyalty and love toward yourself. What I mean by this is that you respect yourself enough not to put your heart, mind, and body at risk. To cheat would be the destruction of self. Cheating is a confessional act of someone too weak to devote themselves to someone else. Cheating is an admission of insecurity.

My heart can't wander because it's invested in someone I genuinely care about. My eyes can't wander because my partner is the only light I wish to see. My body can't wander because my partner is more than enough in the space of comfort and desire. Most men will have you believe that cheating is a part of our DNA, but if anything, cheating is a disease.

So if you've ever been cheated on, first, be grateful that your partner revealed themselves to you as a coward, and second, stay away from those who are unfaithful to your ideas of love and commitment. It is not your fault, and it is not your job to provide an incentive to someone who isn't strong enough to be faithful to you.

I feel strongly about commitment, honesty, and devotion. If you're incapable of all of the above, leave. Cheating is the game of the weak. A game that the strong need not entertain.

meet the Kings.

i know the ugliness of this world

i've felt it in the way my wife's family

pretended to give a fuck about me

i've seen it in their eyes

their gaze staring upon me

thinking of ways

that they can use me or use us

i've seen the color green

on the surface of their intentions

the jealousy in the voices

as they judge me and my wife

for wanting more for ourselves

more than they could ever have

i think my wife's father

blames me for the fracture

in their foundation

and maybe my presence

woke her soul to the disappointment

that has always lived there

but i assure you that i tried

i made an effort, i gave support

i did and continue to do

what others won't

and for that, those relationships

have fallen apart

i've seen the ugliness of this world

and i've seen so much of it

in my wife's family, my family

for yourself.

you moved the rain

you may not have realized it

but you walked toward me

and the closer you got

it stopped storming

and i guess i just want you

to know your power

to realize your magic

and to use that ability

on yourself, for yourself

part six.

Your fear of love began years ago—the absence
of a father, a mother's neglect, and even with the
odds stacked against you. Nothing could stand
in your way of becoming more than they could
teach you to be. And you continue to fight for
everything you deserve, and I want you to know
that I am proud of you.

She moves like a brush to a canvas, a living art form—a profound expression of resistance as she not only fights for what she deserves, she fights against this idea that she should settle. She moves like lightning in search of a space to land. And you either meet her demands or watch her drift away like a dream in the softness of morning.

more self-love

even on your worst days

it's difficult to try for yourself

when you feel broken up inside

but you're learning to continue to fight

there is no light on this earth

that could ever compare to yours

you are a rarity, a sight to be seen

a force to be respected

with a love that should be cherished

don't let them make you feel small

when you were born to be great

Some of you reading this are not in search of
a love that isn't your own, and what I mean
by this is that you're simply looking for more
of yourself. You're trying to find true love in
the details of your existence, and though you
fully deserve to be loved by someone, the most
essential romance is the one you experience
when alone, on your own.

They will envy you, even while concealing
their jealousy. They will look to befriend you,
because the enemy wants to be up close to
witness your downfall and to judge you for all of
your mistakes personally.

_____

The closer you get to certain people, the further
you are from everything you truly deserve. Your
life and the details of your future can often be
altered by the people you spend the most time
on.

It's not that you don't care or that you don't have a heart. You're just good at pretending that it doesn't matter even when it's all you ever think about.

We were warned about strangers and the destruction they cause, but no one told us that most of the pain would come from the people who know us, the people who claim to love us the most. And this is a lesson you learn very early in life—that you must be careful with strangers but even more careful with family and friends.

———————

To find balance, you must find a space that isn't occupied by the people who take from you and never give.

———————

Self-care is saying no to people who don't necessarily deserve a yes.

———————

Peace thrives in the absence of certain people.
Rejoice when the wrong people walk out of your
life.

The ending of any relationship can be difficult, but the fact that it's finally over gives you a greater opportunity to love everything about yourself that they didn't.

———————

chaos is a distraction

a detour from joy

a destroyer of peace

Do not allow your heart to remain in places it won't thrive.

Start telling the truth about family who lie to
you and lie on you.

Your kindness was never a weakness. You were just kind to weak people.

Say no to things that will keep you from living the life you always wanted.

You have always been more than enough, but you have always wanted to be accepted by people who will never be good enough for you. That's the problem. Searching for validation in people who are too stupid to comprehend all that you are.

You have to be willing to walk away from anyone who restricts you from living your best life. This includes family.

A broken woman is a tapestry of strength. The power to conquer and survive are woven beneath her bones and inside her heart and are embedded in her soul.

Phenomenal women are forged in the fires of heartache. And this is how I know that you'll be fine. You feel pain now, but you'll be stronger later. Keep fighting.

you feel broken

you feel discouraged

you feel sadness

throughout your bones

but you are still more

and you are still magic

———————

a love

rooted in devotion

will grow and bloom

and will not wilt

the ocean spends its life

reaching for the shoreline

no matter the distance

no matter the weather

and this is the way love

should be

———————

if the night sky were absent of stars

and the lights from tall buildings ceased

you'd still find your way home

because you, my dear, are the moon

it's tough
but she's learning
how to be alone
she's learning to find balance
in solitude

———————

some days you feel like love

in the spring

and then you turn cold

like the roots midwinter

reduced to strangers

because you could never see

the value in my presence

reduced to shadows

that no longer intertwine

———————

Self-care is ignoring their calls. Self-care is no longer listening to their lies.

she stared into that broken mirror

with a smile laced in tears

because for once

she could truly see herself

for how she felt

i think she stopped looking

to the night sky

when she realized

that she was the moon

and that meant

that she could survive

the midnight hour

———————

the mind says, "fuck you"

but the heart whispers, "i miss you"

———————

if you don't choose her now

you can't choose her later

if you don't love her now

she'll choose herself

and give unto herself

everything you couldn't

and she will find

the delight in your absence

The sadness chases you down at a relatively young age, and you're left to make sense of something that won't make sense to you because you're too young to understand that the pain of loving the wrong person is temporary and the end of one relationship isn't the end of the world.

too late.

please don't fall in love

with anyone who makes you feel

like the love you deserve

is too much to ask for

———————

the first to abandon your heart

is also the one who promised

they'd never walk away from you

again, too late.

please don't go back
to anyone who never intended
to give you a reason to stay

stay, please.

One of my readers wrote me a direct message, and in that message, she explained the pain in her heart, and she asked me not to judge her or to hate her for giving up. I was too late because the following message was a goodbye, and I want her to know that I could never judge her or hate her. I could only have hoped that I could've helped a bit more, and I know that, deep down, she just wanted to escape.

And so, I say this to you, the reader of these words: please stay and allow me to help. Please stay and let life get better. Please stay, because your light is essential, and someone needs it to guide their soul through the darkness you've known. Your light shines so brightly, and it has always been enough to lead you toward salvation. Please stay, because my heart can't take losing someone as mighty as you.

you're damaged

fucked up and broken

but you still deserve a love

that reminds you

that your flaws and imperfections

are what make you lovable

———————

it will never go back

to the way it was

and you will forever be changed

and though this transformation hurts

you will be stronger than you've ever been

so let yourself evolve

———————

stop trying to convince your heart

that it is better off with the one person

who will never know what to do with it

stop trying to convince yourself

that staying and trying harder

will improve a relationship

that isn't meant to get better

Sometimes guys don't even want the person they
broke down. It's a hard truth to comprehend,
but sometimes a guy wants to prove that he
can control someone's heart. And so, for those
of you who wonder how he could hurt you
while proclaiming to love you, this is how, and
someone is reading this now who needed this
message. Be strong and choose yourself. It's
going to take some time, but you are strong
enough to get through this.

———————

Do not build your forever upon the promises of someone who was just searching for a moment.

————————

your heart belongs to you

and this is where it should stay

until you find someone

who loves you in a way

that reminds you to love yourself

you fall out of love

you fall out of friendships

you fall out of a lifestyle

that is unbecoming

of who you wish to be

you fall out of everything

that no longer fits

your idea of peace and joy

and that is okay

it is okay to fall out of spaces

you can't thrive in

———————

don't underestimate the love

of a woman who knows

far too well how it feels

to be broken

You get so wrapped up in how it ends that you miss every opportunity to realize the beauty in beginning again by yourself.

saying sorry

does not shake the fear

nor does it remove

the scars of anguish

an apology

does not end

the suffering

in the mind

One day he'll look back to where he broke you, and you will be gone because you decided not to stay there.

---

nearly dammed and damaged

she used whatever she had left

to be whatever it was she needs

in order to survive again

how the rain feels

when it finds a place

to land

give me that feeling

———————

when your heart is aching

you learn that silence

can be a language

_____

you've had all types of love

except the one that stays

———————

cry an ocean

create a way

to swim away

from him

———————

you're going to be fine

you were built

for this type of breaking

———————————

the thing about drowning

is that you find yourself

reaching for help

from the person

who pushed you in

and held your head under water

———————

eventually their absence

won't make you miss them

their absence will show you

that there is life

without them

she could have anyone

she wanted

and she chose herself

Brokenness is a thing you feel, but it doesn't
have to be your identity.

When you search for true love, peace, and devotion, begin with yourself.

Everyone has baggage. Pack lighter next time.

You have a password for everything except your heart and mind.

———————————

you are a thrill to be with

don't waste your time

being in a mediocre relationship

settling for a mediocre love

scars are stories

not always of horror

some are of survival and triumph

———————

it hurts

but you're still here

you'll make it

you won

not easy.

The phrase "it's easier said than done" will never be a good enough reason to justify being in a relationship with someone who treats you like shit.

Yeah, I get it. Moving on is hard, but don't act like being with the wrong person is easy. You're either going to stay and remain stuck or go and begin to grow.

You keep saying moving on isn't easy, as if staying with someone who treats you like shit is any easier. I just wish you'd begin loving yourself more than you love the one person who will never love you back.

Remember who you were before the heartache began. Remember how it felt before they entered your life. Sure, you were lonely at times, but here you are, all alone, even as they lie beside you. The love was never real, but you cling to them as if something will change. Believing flowers can grow in a garden with tainted soil.

fuck it

you tried

you fought

it hurt

move on

You have to stop chasing behind people who choose to run from you instead of walk beside you. It's time to take everything you have left and give it to yourself. You have to stop forcing people to see something in you they never will.

—————

be with someone

who is as loyal to you

as your shadow

———————

whatever you'll need

you can get it from yourself

You've been feeling the weight of disappointment for most of your life, and I believe that it is time to let go of all the people who continue to let you down. I get it, you're strong, and you've built up a tolerance for pain, but that doesn't mean you deserve to be hurt repeatedly. Just because you can handle it doesn't mean you should put up with it.

You can take all of your loneliest nights and place them next to an evening in bed with someone who hurts you and none of those nights would even compare to the emptiness you feel whenever you share your bed with the wrong person.

You know those moments when you doubt that they'll ever change? The confusion of it all? The fear of starting over and the pain you feel every time you think of your future and the uncertainty of being with that person? Don't ignore it; don't ignore the questions that fill up your heart in the middle of the night when you can't sleep. I promise you, the answer you've been searching for has been with you all along. You know what you have to do.

———————

my wife's big brother

seems so small

the way he never holds

himself accountable

for being absent

from the moments

that really matter

———————

there is something in the wind

whispering her name

the wild calls out to her

"free yourself," is what it says

---

all the silence in her heart screams

she fixed it on her own

she was the savior of her life

be the best thing to ever happen to your own
heart

---

end it

then start over

with all the lessons you've learned

what is fire

without a woman

holding it

a meaningless flame

destined to burn out

winter reaches for her soul

a girl gone cold

rare in ways.

You have always known you were different, but
you have always struggled to find the words
to explain what it is you have seen in yourself.
Your strength unmatched, your will to keep
going, despite whatever sadness you've felt, is
something that could inspire others. See, you've
inspired me to write these words and piece them
together like puzzles to create a picture of you—
an image with warrior-like features and the
demeanor of a Queen. You have always known
you were different, and I've also come to know
the same.

part seven.

I think your intentions are good. You don't want to feel like you're giving up, but in your pursuit to prove your love, you are hurting yourself, and I don't think that's fair. Especially after you've made the effort you've made. It's important to understand that love isn't something you can force. You can't find real love while entertaining fraudulent people. You'll never truly be happy holding on to those who hurt you.

part eight.

What is love if it feels like hatred? What
are promises when they often feel empty?
What is trust when the person you believe in
betrays you? What is an apology when they're
not willing to refrain from the actions they
apologize for? The liar lies, the cheater cheats,
and more times than not, they say "sorry"
without any intention of changing their behavior.
I hope you realize this and do whatever it is you
need to do with this knowledge.

———————

Some breakups involve family. Sometimes you have to move on from the people you thought you needed, especially when they do nothing but keep you further from peace.

part nine.

It's hard, but you're learning to detach from people who show, time and time again, that they are nothing special. You're learning to put distance between yourself and the people who would rather destroy your self-esteem than build you up. That's a lonely place to be; trust me, I know. But your future will illuminate the moment you walk away, and your life's fire will burn brighter as you continue to let go of everything and everyone who doesn't deserve to be kept. I want you to be happy, but more than anything, I want you to know that true happiness is something you can cultivate and maintain on your own. And once you've done this, you'll be able to share that joy with the person who is willing and ready to prove that they deserve to share in your peace of mind.

artwork.

With strokes of madness on a canvas, she made
pain look like art. The way she moved like the
hand of an artist in search of somewhere to land.
An assortment of decisions, both good and bad,
stitched together like pages to the spine of a
book. She's abstract because she's not afraid to
be. Free and wild, filled with magic in a world
that will often be incapable of comprehending
the meaning of why she exists. Framed like the
masterpiece she is, she could live in museums
for all the world to admire. She could go
anywhere in the world if she'd like, and cities of
people would stop to pay homage to her warrior-
like presence. Yes, she could take her aura and
shine it in the middle of the night and make the
dark skies feel like morning. She could be doing
anything in the world, anything she wants, but
she's here at this moment. She is reading this
book, consuming these words. She is you.

reflections.

Look in the mirror and tell the woman you see
that you are proud of everything she has done.
Make a promise to be kinder to her. Look her
dead in the eye and promise her that you will
live your life loving her with all that you have.

So many dreams are painted with lies. They're soft in the beginning, but once you fall, you end up landing on a surface made of stone. You tell yourself that things will change, but the only thing made different are your lips, as you have lost your smile. You begin to break beneath the heaviness of empty promises. You begin to ache in places unimaginable. Your entire future rendered uncertain by the fraudulent character of someone who pretended to love you. This entire event has left you drained, and yet you are full of a form of wisdom that can only reside within the mind and heart of someone who knows what it means to love the wrong person. You learn how to navigate those little fires caused by those who only intend to deceive you. Most times, getting burned is also learning how to survive the flames.

Sometimes I worry about you. Claiming to be
okay, saying "I'm fine" even when your whole
world is burning down. You stand when falling
should be the only option, should lie awake at
night even when your heart needs to rest. You
move on, you move forward as your legs begin
to ache. Searching for everything you lost while
loving someone who decided to hurt you. There
are nights when I worry about you; there are
nights when you fight off the urge to give in, to
give up. There are nights when you just feel like
the darkness is too much and the light from the
moon is not enough, and still you awake the next
morning. Full of strength and hope, despite the
hopelessness that follows you and the exhaustion
you feel for trying to be good enough for
someone who was never good enough for you.
I worry about you, and yet something within
me believes in you and your ability to cultivate
whatever it is you need in order to survive.

The world will always need someone like you. Someone who can show it that, no matter how broken the heart may feel, there is a way to keep going. There is a way to stay alive. You are proof that, no matter what ends, there's a way to begin again.

I've been thinking about you and everything you've faced up until this moment. You are proof of warriors walking the earth disguised as everyday people. You may be a civilian, but most days you find yourself at war with many things, and those things find difficulty in trying to defeat you. Yes, there are moments when you fall, there are moments when you feel like giving up; but instead of giving in, you continue to pick yourself up in preparation for victory. And this is how I know you'll be fine. This is how I know you'll make it, because you always do. You always will. And this is what I think about whenever I think of you.

she whispered and the earth shook

this is the power of a woman

forgiveness does not mean "come back"

––––––––––––

The good memories are excuses to stay,
and lately you've found yourself struggling
to remember those moments. Your body is
beginning to give in to the exhaustion of
fighting to love someone who treats you like
the enemy. Your feet, once hesitant to move, are
now preparing for the tough journey of walking
away from someone you thought you could
never leave. Here you are, reading these words,
a sign of what's to come. A representation of
what you've been feeling. Here you are, in this
moment, growing closer to the idea of letting go.

another goodbye.

You're lost, and you've been searching for yourself for so long. You chose to pick up this book in search of a sign. Maybe you were hoping for some solace, a vacation from the pain you've felt. Perhaps the words in this book triggered a memory, and perhaps you're still trying to remember who you are and what you are capable of in the aftermath of heartbreak.

For whatever reason, my words ended up in your hands and your heart. I hope you figure out how to piece yourself back together again. I hope you find new ways to survive once more and set yourself free from all the pain that has taken up space in your life. I can't promise to have all the answers, but I do know that the most profound answer to everything you've been asking lives within you. You are the hero in this story, you have always been, and I am just the writer who gets the opportunity to remind you of the magic that dwells within all that you are. Please don't give up on yourself. You're so much more than what you may know. And I hope this was a step further in reminding you that the best is yet to come. Take care. Until next time.

index

411

421

she's strong, but she's tired

copyright © 2020 by r.h. Sin. All rights reserved. Printed in China. No part of this book may be used or reproduced in any manner whatsoever without written permission except in the case of reprints in the context of reviews.

Andrews McMeel Publishing
a division of Andrews McMeel Universal
1130 Walnut Street, Kansas City, Missouri 64106
www.andrewsmcmeel.com

22 23 24 25 26 SDB 10 9 8 7 6 5 4 3

ISBN: 978-1-5248-5828-5

Library of Congress Control Number: 2020930788

Editor: Patty Rice

Art Director/Designer: Diane Marsh

Production Editor: Elizabeth A. Garcia

Production Manager: Cliff Koehler

attention: schools and businesses
Andrews McMeel books are available at quantity discounts with bulk purchase for educational, business, or sales promotional use. For information, please e-mail the Andrews McMeel Publishing Special Sales Department: specialsales@amuniversal.com.